is a door

Fred Wah

Talonbooks

Copyright © 2009 Fred Wah

Talonbooks
PO 2076, Vancouver, British Columbia, Canada V6B 3S3
www.talonbooks.com

Typeset in Sabon and printed and bound in Canada on 30% post-consumer recycled acid-free paper.

The publisher gratefully acknowledges the financial support of the Canada Council for the Arts; the Government of Canada through the Book Publishing Industry Development Program; and the Province of British Columbia through the British Columbia Arts Council and the Book Publishing Tax Credit for our publishing activities.

Library and Archives Canada Cataloguing in Publication

Wah, Fred, 1939–
Is a door / Fred Wah.

Poems.
ISBN 978-0-88922-620-3

I. Title.

PS8545.A28I82 2009   C811'.54   C2009-902841-7

to the dogs

Dear Bear,
Be aware,
this door
should make you
stop and stare.

Mostly fir
and pretty thick,
the bark is gone
but the scent is fixed.

Dear Dogs,
Late at night
our hunger
is a love
that bites.

Kick it open
make it slide
where's a door
we haven't tried.

Contents

ISADORA BLUE

Isadora Blew

Isadora blew and blew the sea the sand the blue boards sky high waves smashed broke and splintered shutters white walled water over roof (it's true!) and filled the floor with beach roar blues but you'd be too to start the day as blue sky-blue could fool you too now look at the misery you can see right through poor sad and lonely one she knows you'll spend your nights alone and never know how much nobody's missed somebody's blue yeh! ain't this storm come through my door tellin' you

Forwords

forwords or
that's old
rocking life
from trike
to chair's got
last night's
ancianos bird
on america's
fraying wire

's africa
of whose
countenance
as peeled
dis content
signals core
or gated roof
another lust
forever rust

Five Peelings Waiting

for Richard Baillargeon & Salvador Alanis

1.

After I kicked the wall so hard my leg recovered its kitchen.
A hinge then a horizontal expression.
Morning just finished what's missing from the white cafe.
First the agua caliente and then pay up.

2.

He had a touch of Winnipeg.
But just across the park strolled Tinisima's ghost.
And then she longed for the island of untouchable logging.
Later we'd all get lost.

3.

First fix the word to the thing.
Only the coffee is cold (*dictamen condensare*).
When the plaza is the last still place.
We'll get back the map of printing.

4.

Next to Gaia's the repair shop.
So we had cervezas and watched the walls talk to the city.
The shadows fell behind the shutter.
Between you something's missing —

5.

Lost processes of reconnaissance.
Last imagenes.
Lost sentences.
Last objects the lost scene seen.

Ordinary Itching Poem in Trans

Just like white gauze
Forget the world

White-headed crows

Only dew,
Therefore grass

Moon meticulous,
The sound of ten thousand branches,
Therefore rivers, pines

The radical
Plums,
In heaven's refrigerator

Late spring, early autumn
Diving or pissing so late at night
A watchman
And bowl of wine
Silence clear as music

Ratio to remember
Axe to handle
Too far off

Walking Poem
for Don Gill

Look into the magic ground before each step and feel the grounding cord
trailing behind as a tail anchored to earth then shift the gaze to see those
parts of the world you were prevented from glimpsing by the laws of sitting
still in thought circling cinematically in motion these virtual plains of the
eyes and cellular history there on the pavement or gravel in front of you the
dry grass without water and the way it flows in comfort not regret only the
easiest most restful way except this can be difficult this resistance of walking
through choice while not always in control of the adverb recording each step
as a past event or even remembering magic but not some other system of
positioning a taste for the local and for this fortress of solitude that ambles
its own imperfect clock sweeping your music head down in a pilgrimage of
archival string.

Sheet Music

for Charles Bernstein

Why did they say eliminate the negative
transparency, don't mess with Mr. In-Between
or pandemony? Sit tight and close low
right down to the maximum, some
latch for an onto, maintaining
a plus from a pulse. Well then
illustrate:

latch onto the nexus while claiming the crux
of the squall. The positive also equals
the page. Ok, I'll take the floor, a
blendable family, double-U-Ay-Aych
aching. Positively, adverb or not
could be more than the accent outside
immigration — who
cares if it does? Doing weather except

why apply for the job if
the hinge isn't broken? I have
stolen the report and now can't find
a door, just when I need one. Even
a sliding door. Side-to-side cloud

thought Noah the dark thought
Jonah what did they do
except wait away and never let
go? My joy's spread, my maximum's
lost interest. Otherwise you'll be other
you know, you'll be background,
and that makes the word
the door with difference:
doored.

The downburst blows away, the scene
affirmative by the day. Word's out
what I need to do is mess around
with Mister In-Between.

The Marlin Seafood Grill
for Laura Barrón

It's called the Marlin for two reasons. First, I had this stuffed marlin of my father's. He got it when he worked in Mexico after leaving China around 1902, before he came to Canada. But I also wanted to call it the Marlin to honour my father's brother, uncle Mah Lin, who was murdered in Calgary in 1900. His death was one of the reasons my father had to leave home in China. Mah Lin was murdered in the spring of 1900 by a young boy, the son of the woman he worked for in Calgary. He was only nineteen years old and my father, that year, was just sixteen. An old Chinese proverb says, "If one who attains honour and wealth never returns to his original place, he is like a finely dressed person walking in the dark." Mah Lin had been buried in Calgary but the family wanted his remains, his bones, to bury him next to his ancestors. At that time there were companies in North America that were involved in the business of returning bodies, but our family couldn't afford to, so they decided to send my father to Canada to get his brother Mah Lin's bones. My father had to work his way across and the first work he got was on a boat going halfway around the world to the Caribbean. But he also liked to gamble too much and he ended up cooking in a restaurant in Mérida in the Yucatán for a couple of years before he earned enough to get passage to Canada. He made it to Canada in 1904 but the Head Tax was so high he ended up without money and had to find work. At first he cooked on the boats around Vancouver. But he also liked to bet on the horses so his gambling habits kept getting in the way of recovering Mah Lin's bones from the graveyard in Calgary. He got involved in a bunch of different Chinese cafes in western Canada and, after he married a white woman, my mother, a cashier in one of his cafes, he never did finish the job he was sent to Canada to do. That was left to me and it wasn't until 1951, a few years after they changed the Chinese Exclusion Act in 1947, that I was able to get Mah Lin's bones and take them back to China. I met a few people still living from his family but they were still so poor I gave the bones to the Kwan Family Association, which was happy to bury them in the family graveyard near Canton. But when anyone comes into the Marlin Seafood Grill here in Banff, they think that big fish on the wall is the real name of this restaurant. But for me and our family it's the Mah Lin. We thought of calling it Chinaman's Peak after that mountain in Canmore, but people here are still a little prejudiced so we thought it wouldn't be such good luck for business. Besides, seafood in Banff, in the mountains, is a real treat, a specialty. You gotta do things that are good luck, even if you're not a gambler. Like that umbrella up there on the wall, that's good luck too. My half-cousin in Mérida sent that to me; it was her wedding umbrella. She married a Japanese guy and in Japan it's good luck to be married under an umbrella. It's from Japan, but the white people here just think we're all the same. Once in awhile, on Fridays, we serve *Marlin à la Marlin*; it's really swordfish but even that's getting hard to find this far north.

Double Dutch

I was standing in the doorway
Not doing any harm
When along came the nation
And took me by the
Hinges in my history
The key inside my cock
And gave me a passport
To pass me through their door
Way back in Swift Current
Down by Speedy Creek
Where they gave me a name
And their social numbers
I could never add 'em up
So it's hard to skip to
Lemon coke soda
Chicken salad lunch
Tell me the name
Of your honey
Bunched up in the middle
Being in between
Caught inside the doorway
Not wanting to be seen
Not in or out
Not on either side
Just a boy scouting for
That big sugar doughnut
Frozen tongue on top
Tell me who's your sweet
Ache at the heart of
Spanish dancer, do the splits
Spanish dancer, kick the door
Along came "stay there"

Part of a little notion to
Keep standing in the doorway
Minding the commotion

Hey, Man!

Juan José he
is valid
he sings
all the way
to Valladolid.

What's that he said
"polloco"?
Or did he say we saw
the zapalote.

Hey, Man!
he's a buzzard
with his bones
all over his shirt
on the way
to Chemax.

And he speaks fast
the real stuff.
Let's take a taxi
to Tixcacal Tuyub.

He says his uncles
are his mother's brothers
saying, singing
with that bottle in his hand
he's ringing.

Wind him up
with movies, books
handsome smile

in his white Jipijapa.
Hey, Man!
he's the one
from Mazatlán.

I need to apply Canclini here

I need to apply a soft pedal
for entering and leaving
the dark street of "The Aleph"
lit dim by traditional values
while the valves of Nuevo gringo
capitalize the conversation
languageless in the conversion.

The stem of the familiar local,
that local white shirt there, disappears
as it neons through a door.

I had wanted to meet with Mariana
Estrada Castillo. Mestizaje
our own Miss Edge in Nation.
Restore the language of mixed verbs
not the dashboard of codes
designed with intention.

But she wasn't home.
She's reinvested
in the symbolic good.

Hammering
of the jake brakes purr
out on the city limits.
The descent beckons.

Coke's winning here.
Come home with the camshaft,
confess to the missing.
Not diet but dying.

Logging In

for Humberto Suaste

We looked for openings along the shoreline or old driftwood rafts where we might get out for a clean cast. Either the alder or small spruce grew right down to the edge or it was a shallow bottom of silt. The only deep pools were under steep, high rocks. But then, at the south end of the lake, just before it emptied into its alpine creek, I found an old deadfall held out of the water by some rocks and relatively steady. It had a few patches of slippery moss here and there but mostly it was dry so I could walk out to the end of it and get a good cast into fairly deep water just above the mouth of the creek. At first I tried a spinner, a "Deadly Dick," but it was a still day and the cutthroat weren't going for it. Then I tried a bobber, six feet of leader, and a fly, a "Coachman." That did it. I pulled about eight or nine out of that spot in less than half an hour. The end of the log was also a good place to clean them, so I did, throwing the offal back into the water so the bears wouldn't start hanging around this log. That log had become a partner and I can see its gracious gesture of falling along the shore as a kind of gift, an amulet, a dowsing rod of weathered possibility.

On Second Thought
20 Answers for José Teodoro

1.

Yes, as I was driving west on King Ed
through the intersection at Dunbar
in Gladys's Rambler rambled
thought became a "thunk."

2.

I couldn't describe "relaxing"
nor is it sometimes
"stressful" "it"
being an "isness"
a kind of floating referent
just like "there"
and its "arenesses."

3.

If "Memory" really "is a kind of
... renewal" and "change"
is supposed to be at rest,
music is the heart of thinking,
the knock of the name upon the door,
then maybe the liver be a fire
or envy flush, a hand
could be to count on?

4.

The kindling was as wet
as an accomplishment.

5.

Imagine an engine can
take the ra out of "brain"
an instant "bin."

6.
Only beautiful horses
or happy hogs
careful horses
or snappy dogs
iffy horses
sniffing for frogs

7.
Not so bitter
that lyingness of adverbs.
when the protagonist droops
but goes on to the sudden end
bitten.

8.
Yes,
my dog isn't so little
but she follows her name
just as any word
would another.

9.
For some reason
I start at the waist,
though I realize now
that's changed with age;
in my twenties
it would have been
the ankles being
whatever wants to be thin
and held.

10.
You need a nickel
to play the song
so jimmy the lock
to hear Emily sing
carefully an Oh!

11.
To "illuminate" a point
is like turning a planet
into a metaphor,
ineffable into a fable,
inging stones across the water
or the lake wood or metal.

12.
I think it was winter
it was raining
perhaps November
(though maybe January
— it depends)
No, I'm unsure
was it in a boat
a rowboat
a wooden one
summer, then
or late summer
just before
returning to school
you know
that time of year
when belief sets in

but an exact time
is what we want of the spirit
or else it's less than more
which makes it spring
a northern spring
barely there at all
but widely, then.

13.
skeleton Caribbean
full protection suit
first time or first truth
the word coast
looks back.

14.
Same thing:
8-year-old logs
stationary
bike.

16.
Counting.
But I have to make up the question.
Yes, you must become a slave
to your own hand over fist.

17.
Not so strange
you should ask.
I was thinking about it
just yesterday —

where are my father's ashes?
Stone
would be nice.
Words a'scatter.

18.
And greens.
Bok choy
after the Salvation Army.
Family matter.
Remember mouth.

19.
Kootenay Lake.
Creek's
Mouths.

20.
Talk radio
Deutsche Welle
's twin
Sleep.

is a door

is a door wood

is a door a board

is a door barred

is a door abhorred

is a door locked

is a door shocked

is a door cut

is a door shut

is a door a jar

is a door nailed

is a door split

is a door fixed

is a door hung

is a door stripped

is a door bolted

is a door supposed

is a door closed

is a door broken

is a door spoken

is a door a word

Mr. In-Between

I was walking on the beach
after Isadora
at Telchac Puerto
where all the broken doors
are *las puertas rotas*.

Between *puerto* and *puerta*,
The port and the portal
Portage and Main
The Spanglish in anguish
Before and after
The Sass- in disaster
Between the beach and the water

the pandemonium of passage
iterates a constant supercell
of ignition, how to hang on
in a wedge of vortex free from shear
and the siren of echo
how to find the door
to stand in the way
just be there Mr. In-Between

ETHNOGY JOURNAL

Hotel Comfort Jan 10

Bones bound matrix
The Resurrection
of the selected world
organic now humid
air close to soul-stuff
some courier animal
William Blake parent
of jumbo jet fact
chosen the body
chooses words such as
saying "from within"
that parabola "ph"
wanting streetwise epithets
to fossilize the marketplace
metal roof shimmers
across from Hotel Comfort
sweet trucks sit
in the warehouse courtyard
nothing, especially poetry,
will get in the way, don't
want the neck to know
its own massage.

(was) Monday Jan 11 Samui

Stomach cessing
search for lost twin
split intestinal
marrow reading channel
tractor stuck some
furrow lurched day
outside (expect
the cramp, pain
and potent typical
assemblage so-called
overwhelm

Tuesday Jan 12 Samui

but the rain fate
some kind of inner magnet
wet, long, and alien
Asian road with clouds
guiding the electrical stove
stuff brought time
the uniform of school
can hardly comply
with the geography
that guides these democratic
souls to accommodate pattern
keeps falling into the same old
deep hole in the sidewalk. Today
shoot nothing but green.

Samui Wed Jan 13

The Beach Leonardo di
something boy film
as children do, grains
that sandpaper feet bottom
footprint, toes sink bound
the child's capacity
to rust.

Sun circles shadow
as a series of strategies
for skin not clear
about goodness
walked down sentenceless
to the end and back
plastic and shell struggle
rope debris what if
this beach is the hospital?

Friday Jan 15

as well. happy. at
the sunshine, and coasted
into the whole leaf
waving, pea-pod green
perfect shells my large
emotional agenda a giveaway
dark so soon, friction
not just sand
seek the one seat
next wave
to sit on. so
scattered.

Monk scroll

Plans for the interior, the language all 'round cut or can't get a grip but ok to
let blur happen talk of getting spiffed-up Sunday morning as if to match every
street paved just because yesterday they spent all afternoon at the noodle house
talking about movies they've seen simply to validate the edges of non-thought
who'd wait to fall into the abyss or even pay the taxes.

Sunday morning dark

Tried blunt jackfruit
thud excerpt from the trees
river and falling about
bamboo forearms bitten
crashed and split,
pregnant fig floats opium
brown full rains large
imaginary birds cartwheel
"cut — don't cut"
all down the line
buddhite minding the hoot
colouring into the long night
sudden travelling in transmission
flack shift
next thought
last

Missing Monday sandy

Numbered thinking
perception patience memory —
a light order? Andaman,
Thai spitzes, breakers
from here to Bangkok
net done to leaky rooms
jungle and sun not so
little anglo-saxon euro
topless tropics then
"clouds like feathers"
Poseidon chicken picnic
back over tided sand
sighted while looking
for memory's cracks
that silly man's a, b, sea.

Wed Jan 20

On the boat to Ang-Thon Marine Park a young man holds up his Grundig
video camera so I guess German farang Thai gay couple — Thai guy holds up
a Sony. I take a photo of a fisherman working in another boat. Take his work.
Does colour have a social value, I ask. Of course, she says.

Na Thon Nation Sunday Jan 24

New streets Na Thon
nation fist close to the breadth
of its circling cycles
breathing thin
revved and spitting on
fat attic of tourist shops
people crawl in and out
of more-more America
uncurious and cotton
apple of their eyes

Thurs Jan 28

some carrier of an anecdotal jet
like that coffee shop
food as photo
just a monk
saffron

the sentence
as the tunnel of love
intend to put the words together
make them thicker

the present participle looking up
through the jungle canopy
by the man who said
he was hard to dry.

Jan 28.2

(Butterfly mobiles of coral. Ex-pat
Irishman with German experience
now owns own mangosteen farm
just 40k south from here.)
Another fist to close the circle
kickstand scraping
alphabet a mere "sea-green"
conditional of a Chinese-Belgian
choice on the street menu
"Noodle Pour Down with
Strong Soup Vegetable"
some bias or bayou
record du jour.

Later Jan 28.3

(National parks invisible
gibbons ou-ou, ou-ou
right to the edge of the river).

Across the boundary, shade
green photo dug in
Khao Sok NP.

So she didn't walk very far
could and these very nice breezes
her breasts' presentness and pretty.

A one canopy mindfulness
The Emptiness of Saying
tubed down river.

But when she did
it was through a forest of rice
mouth full of talk
always hungry.

Night Jan 28

European touch of tropic —
real rainforest under rain

undrowned sounds of
cicadas frog fronds

order is last up
things like leaves lip

now think over dry season
very composed canopies

but order in the precepts
how hollow or how full

Friday Jan 29 Morning

Preceptual order of flora
outside yet to the west
We had picked up leeches
thigh and back then
blood poured
from under her watch strap
is that the tool box of love
copyright of leaves, ferns, etc.
but it got a little boring
photography can make it new
another grammar to walk through
break the rule of coagulation
the borders of the garden
cross-trails just turn around
come back whole truth
nothing but mourning.

Evening before 30 quiet

Being where
overwhelming scars
screams and frogs
attention to the mud
of mind embroidered shy
broken branches thatch
swells plop of teak fake
tin flowers incessant
twitter of varnished board
rot ping-pong table-top
made from bamboo slats
unpredictable here
there every
where.

Poseidon Bungalows Jan 30

Tried their boat owl-like
noodles blunt practising bluntest
against the world nouns.
Poseidon Bungalows' wells
dry so early this afternoon
to the sea then pretty green
hear the gibbons head down
that dried out hoot Buddhist
rule against killing dull or limp
shoal of every morning hunt
for water-slap sound
but never see them waiting
at the bus station.

Wedding

Tussle and rest deal with the gut in the morning truck ride to the airport cold numb hands now sit in the sun and wait for the 11 a.m. flight to arrive adze to ridgepole two days left less demanding someone at Starbucks says they're trying to figure out the next move lots of dissonance slash and burn maybe the municipality is in the clear.

Khao Lak Sunday Jan 31

The Brit family leaves the beach. Long-tail boats far away. The reef arrives /
from morning tide. The size of the sand matters. That's the navy — they
don't like you and you can't see them. Boy with plastic bottle runs to the
shore. Bamboo driftwood. UV rays under the skin. Hot coffee on the "cafe
lawn." Young girl wears jeans and long t-shirt swimming. More broken Nike
sandals litter the beach than ... Tropic vs. topic. Like a breath of hot air. Like
the neighbourhood bar. Like a modern setting. Like a new factory. Like a
last resort.

Sunday still

world daily sculpt
to coast, song tow periphery
each departmental thought
a coherence of flow files
called "home" check agenda
cut grass, motor's
trying to teach me something
if I could find a shadow
record the floor tiles — ape
the moment, how much
does that Honda Wave cost?
Then take it back.

Tuesday Feb 2

German — maybe Swede then my Honda's
beauty if UV skin deep in the climate machine's
dream down at 125 cc a piece of rebar w/ two
loops welded near the top the beach umbrella
bobs the word "boat" w/ its long-tailed diesel
want one and I want it home on Kootenay Lake
or pick up one of those "Ethno-G" Casios across
the table she says are you Chinese or Japanese?
My story just won't end.

Thurs Feb 4 Bangkok

She's eating the durian w/ nose puckered
papain! papain! from the plastic bag no
chopsticks gratis south of the city of angels,
if we could only grow bamboo at lake
level it's morning and her eyes lilt (from
"slit") when they talk politely almost dart
across one of my race oceans there! my
white she covers her mouth when she laughs
"Workaholic since 1967 — Gray Zone" I shoot
maybe 2 or 3 rolls a week is that ice safe
to drink (or ski on) "my life"
on the t-shirt that doesn't seem to be a sentence.

Thursday night

European trout
rain furtive
listening
history's silent
downpour landscape chalk
caves and islands
infiltrates 19th century
order no compost
the future jungle home
to the rough touch
trans-local and not cloud
continental distance
just my difference
stream static, all of it
used to catch
attention, practise saying
"toilet"
practise saying
"our Jungle House."

Feb 6 Saturday

Where's that skin from if not hide to cover shade of brown complex.
Dark enough to still the translocal islands of "our" people.
That arm's white enough to be on the bus burning.
Gold chain complement.
Black hair tan face no fantasy.
Blond dreadlocks and a Thai sarong.

Sunday sunny too

This city takes too much trim
Get into chopping
Road its toll
Boot on the body

Zena, Wave, & Dream parked
One 25 cc Dragon-tail boat
River under Honda
Amex Om the safe.

Bangkok Feb 10 clear

Hand to handle then to mouth
pollution time taken from the lunch
(or lungs)
just hire me for that dicté
this end of the city hungrier
(or mess)

cafe life each meal
so much someone else's
(kitchen)

not know what to get
choice natters need
(or pay up)

Could be Friday

And then they decided the war's
over quickly packed it up again
and moved to Tawa in that
they rotate parts
stay permanent but they need
whatfor those young people
who do karaoke
that's the blindest life
"I sing," they say
we don't have places to go
my life's compact
and basically like badminton
is very popular
but doesn't make much sense
so it's why you go to the states
there's very little
for them to do
here's where you mix
entertainment with silence
but we have museums
and now all over the world
that's the direction they go
but they need more sports
to take their minds off.

DISCOUNT ME IN

Race, to go

What's yr race
    and she said
what's yr hurry
how 'bout it cock

                asian man
I'm just going for curry.

        You ever been to ethni-city?
        How 'bout multi-culti?

        You ever lay out skin
        for the white gaze?

What are you, banana
or egg? Coconut
maybe?

        Something wrong Charlie
        Chim-chong-say-wong-leung-chung?
        You got a slant to yr marginal eyes?

You want a little rice with that garlic?
Is this too hot for you?

        Or slimy   or bitter   or smelly   or tangy   or raw   or sour

— a little too dirty

        on the edge   ~~hiding underneath~~   crawling up yr leg   stuck

between the fingernails?

Is that a black hair in yr soup?

> *Well how you wanna handle this?*
> *You wanna maintain a bit of différ-ence?*
> *Keep our mother's other?*
> *Use the father for the fodder?*

What side of John A. Macdonald's tracks you on anyway?

> *How fast you think this train is going*
> > *to go?*

Count

Trust me, I was somewhere
else. In 1947 I don't think
I was counted. I must have
been Chinese. From the summit
of myself I was on the other side,
part of an exclusion act. Wonder
if the census counted my mother
as another Swedish ghost, my half
self already paying down the Social
Insurance Number so hard to remember.
Just look it up, again and again
the numbers get jammed, the lock
tumbled into the Family Universe Index.
I didn't know where I was
always ending up somewhere else,
floated over Saskatchewan west with the vote
a British Columbian Subject still living
outside of the state, un countable since
birth.
      I keep looking for a signifier
to cling to. These days iteration
might not find me home except
it's late and I want to play
my part post-immigration, the shadows
of numbers to include the click-clack
of Mah-jong above Pender, casinos
of NAFTA still busing the loot
24 hours a day to International
Village. Global count a digital Olympics
so you can trust me I'm
usually somewhere else the census catches
up and so does the vote
re counted and be caught.

Me

Charlie Chim Chong Say
Wong Leung Chung John
no Jim he says first to remember
Henry and his dad walking down
Granville Street first heard of Ghengis
Khan you remember that'd make the
grandfather a son called Kwan Foo-lee
that is Jim says you know
Kuan Yü of epic San Kuo
I tell Doctor Aung not Mah
my dad was really Soon.

Remember nothing immigration man
across the table you may sit
and make the name a mind
a stamp upon these disappearing
slanted eyes no Charlie left to Chan
the movie or the memory find
your name is my name our name
leftover slash of bones alone
leftover commander front-to-back
after sign in Chinatown slowly
call again he spell me off
he sigh him as a middle name
official smile hey you
who me?

In

In Hum
humiliation
Hum however
Hum heavy birthday
Dominion Hum
Except/Accept
Hum libre, liberalize
Hum hefty head tax
Hum go back
where you came from
Hum the acts
Hum immigration
Hum exclusion
Hum citizenship
Hum enemy alien
Hum Komagata Maru
Hum subject British
Hum citizen white
no yellow Hum
cheap labour
Hum husbands and fathers
Hum ex and ex
taboo the tea girl
in your cafe
Hum however again
However waves and waves
Hum horde
Hum yellow peril
Hum white sugar
Hum white blue-collar
but include within the hum in "in"
the shout of "out!"

Writing

"   *purity of all things seen*
through the   thrust
forward   the vehicle
container   or "thing" called body
because time   appears
to look
   through them   the   nutrient creeks
where was never the problem animal is
   still
with a sigh"
                    never longed for
language on Baker Street nickeled and
dimed to death for the blended
white social justice totemed the city's
parking meters that kind of household
growth not a promise just anxious
foot on the pedal out of
there some map subconscious bucket
with hole turns out to be
actual and not some form-filled
citizenship that just happened to be
someone else's complete thought never tried
to cut the gap in town
except at least three times out
along Ymir Road, that was still
fresh to be *where* anyone could
point to the class projects right
here in town: the lumber mill,
CPR, the Ministry of Mines and
Resources, and a Court House covered
in vines, yet our kitchen talked
back, allowed the door's

the gap that's the aim, design
a sentence that breathes its own
intransitive sigh

Public

The public wall for a few
private souls as *the* poetics (Olson,
Poetry New York no. 3, 1950) spoken
by the wall though never much
heard even if you feel language
serves the you who speaks but
who is the boss of your single
intelligence and all of these questions
return dream after dream and, as
poets, we might stumble on common
readings as the line turns back
to the wall at the left
marginalization of poetry or are Perelman's
words just another benign discursion counting
this poem also as the arbitrary
factory of public opinion churns out
another survey just as those global-
local logics spin the daily papers
as "us," we've become the news
of our "selves" is that your
dream of a public language? Davidson's
own "tentative intervention into the power
grid"[1]
and Derksen's call to designate
"the site of intervention" into "the
long neoliberal moment"[2]
but such thought
is not the line that turns
to complete itself but a "gap"
un defined by its walls, public
language is not the common Creeley
hoped for, the Zócalo's another sign

for whose town plan, the poem
has too long sat down by
the banks of logic's river and
chanted me oh my, whose tears
of privacy and territory are whispers
up against the crying wall another
unheard public on the other side.

1. Michael Davidson. "The Dream of a Public Language: Modernity, Manifesto, and the
   Citizen Subject" in *Xcp: Cross-Cultural Poetics* 17, 2007: 72–88.
2. Jeff Derksen. "Introduction" to "Poetry and the Long Neoliberal Moment" in *West Coast
   LINE* 51 vol. 40, no. 3, 2006: 4–11.

Selves

Selves is a plural noun dormant within the outside though it is not a pronoun so when *I* chatter *we* don't get colder

it tricks language into an intense recitation of *I we I we I we* as a way to keep warm around the pockmarked tongues of other selves

a translation of winter that comes after winter

left holding the math of multiple history

just like Lorca's ghosts the frogs of South America are wide awake

see, this is how difficult post-hibernation gets when plurality reveals its linguistic DNA, when the Great Vowels shift and all the pronouns splash into the pond like single green needles

shiver under the perfect presence of after

Between You and Me There is an I

Between two stools
The hyphen lies
The eggs and the nest
The blind and the fold
The hinge of the city
The door and the jamb
The map and its edges
The wars I've not fought
The life and its lease
The rope but which end
The brink and disaster
The bank and the laughter
The spike below Chinaman's Peak
That spot where the two rails meet

From between two stools
Hear the silence rise
The smoke 'round your neck
The tongue and the dash
The cat and the cradle
The dog dead in the creek
The slash and the burn
The shadows of NAFTA
The head and the tax
Rock bluff and river
The laundry its mark
The height and the trestle
Cata and strophe
Not caboose but what's after

Reference

Let me assemble a line that simulates the working day.
Let my history tell you what I mean.
Neutralizing the novel doesn't settle anything.
Commodity needs a new theory like a stick needs life experience.
Just because we've inherited a quarter section of speech.
Let me remind you how to raise a buck.
Let me be the detection device, a parged cabbage wafting in from subalternville.

tOOl fOOd 1

The connection of handle
To blood is obvious
Pass the tensile nouveau screw
Straight skirts in the pantry
A feast of hereness and thereness
Memory reaches container status
Tupperware those bits
Cut those oats in half
With the steel that feeds whereness
Cup it and cap it
Mark it with "OO"
Stuff it in the drawer
As a history of stew

tOOl fOOd 2

This bench is the consequence of a so-called citizenship of consumption. Ands ifs or buts should be used to modernize eating on the go, i.e. eating on the job. And the site of this decadence of weekend Tom-toolery in the past decade seems outside the civil and the social. If this house of tools rehearses the illusion of the "how to build a wind turbine" project to question the value of "unfinished business," then who, at this late stage, can understand the alien or the aleatory. But this manic oscillation between hand and mouth, between stomach and stud wall, ("Learn Hypnosis Today") after thirty weekends of attempting to construct alternatives to such planned menus of migration, have left us with nothing more than a new saw blade, a new line snapped but after opening the late afternoon beer.

tOOl fOOd 3

The sun was hot. Lunchtime.
He left his tools on a rock. Plumbing plastic.
She said "spanner." He knew he was dealing with a Brit.
Sardines, grilled and bony. A glass or two of Douro.
Wrench, he said. Crescent!
An eight ok? Ok.
Pingado. Por favor.

tOOl fOOd 4

Set the table
Clear the table
Wipe the table
Go to the table
Not at the table
Head of the table
Under the table
À table

I left it for you on the table

A single brick "why"
Crashes its proof
Into the domestic cup

Everyone's hungry
And wants to come home

Naturalized Citizen Peeled

Last processes of reconnaissance
lost imagenes much difficult.

Re- cognition is a process for equally lost sentiments realizing unswerved
de-sweeping of lost objects,

does come in the end of the characteristic principals dust
national though different.

Opaque

      Amalgam ache me-
tis   rite to exit   syncrude
      durable syncretic symbolism
massified modernism   trans-
      urban vanguard man   is
thetic
       collection plate
                 multitemporal hetero-
gene (the Bride of Cuba)
       lack of time   imbalanced
camshaft
         ethnovideo mexicanness War
     misced op
local bifurcation unconscious or unintentional ambiguity
         raza razor
the real middle can leave at any time
      either you or me, we could be the devilery boy
rootless but dirtless
             total local practice
third word
      ism

Rubble

as if
skin

left
nicked

half a
body

listen
up

ninety
percent

dark
matter

other
radicals

between
the pieces

after
the message

just leave.

HINGES

Abdijection
for Roy

desperate the fact
that the verb waits
to act at the end
of the sentence

to still think on feet
one of those sweet
bouquets green grass
bent into mud

pierced tools a "me"
holds onto
the years as an exercise
in syntax

the foreign sound
of someone else's
motor grinding
a shared sadness

communal consonants
hum of the core semiotic
"we" that *feels* the archive
behind the wheel

tread of tire or foot
black rubber shadow
mimics the emperor's
overcoat and hat

the mud of British
Columbia's spring

epic breakup hollow
board walking

doesn't mean a thing
even as complete thought
parks itself in a circle
to predict the predicate

"I can't understand it
if you don't feel like talking."
Empty, or run on empty?
Race, or bet on raceway?

Grey sky's turned black
you're one of "they"
Just turn your back
and walk away.

He's not his photo
He's not his car
He's not that Happy
Land that's gone to war.

Surrender's just the verbal
sign to raise your arms.
The sentence exercise
to touch your toes.

Aporia

the loop of his death
Septembers a smoke of resistance
mountains too, the town milled

elephantine in the episteme
(nice word) get it
toxic page dying logic

his body knows the time
why I am the space slowed down to breathing
Dostoevsky's metaphor

the valley could be my lung
when I die "I" doesn't
you get it

all the air a flight from Mt. Soma
never know aporia
nor get past *his*-es impasse

Beg to be

anomalous we had named the Dorises
work that needed immediate "longing"
    clean up this place and move on
    dumpsters full of spent chunks

                  the car
used, said "try together" suss your name out front
    walk looking for some aroma, stumble

                      this loss

      late terra we had come to
    that was about 1953 then

              unfull

uncut fuss, stuck

"Bright light of the shipwreck"
for Peter

held
> to be wild

as to be crosschecked
> by the many

eachness always intact
> *for* any dialect

any torrent
any litters
any long plural stoop

boneless potatoes
"common sense"
of the streetlamp

that's the truth
about melodies
the universal ones

who live among the beaches
> and nurse

scrape scrape, a long day for the workmen and a long day for their women waiting for their soft passion, oh, to spend the next day nesting. Just far enough from Hastings to enjoy the silences of your residential fold, far enough from the container cranes, just far enough from the supply depots of relevance, the symbols *for* "being numerous."

Calypso Lille

To begin with, no one in the town slept as Ocean terraced thought overlapping coal seams with night vision surrounded by a pine-spruce forest and soft moss where She could play out her edges of lip down a long, wide, white-rose apron spotted with purple and crowned with a plume of yellow hairs open to the spume and crash of shakuhachi shore and warmth of cheek.

Class

I have tried to shape the meeting
but it has been a mute doting
on new work.

The kohlrabi along the cedar fence
appendage of age.

The drawing to dismantle the pass
is to rhetorize the sieve of possibility.

Like a little green blade of Spanish,
the curriculum so Reaganite.

Given this gathering's almost able
to use marmoleum as a grudge.

Grassroots thought the subaltern
catalogue of opposition.

What a travesty of access,
fighting words among the camps.

Clematis Creek Humming

columbia virgin's bower: bell rue and horse gate to the creek world above Crowsnest cut off the clit or horns of heaven some pale purple tree-river honing home and the twig torn with meaning to sign pale purple (chocolate on the trunk of the pine tree) climbing climbing into you stem limp at your musk to cop petals this tongue pepper and the gorge in an outfall of brown spring runoff the slope coal cloned to the mat of this dusk's sepal delta deep touched tooth your butter my cup

Defend the Zero

I don't know
if they're worth the money
quieter than forever

that's the "new" style
we have doctors
in tears, right

but you're the client
as far as you're concerned
you're a best buy

a handy brand
promptly, promontorily
burning up, toast.

Frank Slide Harebell

campana hanging
blue bell stylus
erect

and elevated
(earth moving)

could be that fingered keel
tuft of anther tip

foreshaded night
moan behind the knee
(knots) seeds

and long
but lips

say *ula*
bladed tonguefish
(memory coming home
uvular)

ankles sheathed
tight yet wet
could be slender
harmony of water
threaded clapper
ringing

memory coming home
to creek bell.

Head Smashed In

The "I" might be simple
Located down the line
To fall wake up
Old log trips
Limb is to stub, bark as to chain

Don't think social norm or lex
Leg's on the cliff too
Manna on the bushes
Not up nor back down
So many extra universal joints

Clothe nothing with preps
Whose syntax is no bone
Spit differential syntax
The larch hurts more
Law capitalized meaning

Self-vex your self as salt
Tongue acrid and stuck
Middle voice emptied
This bruise these stones
The way out thought Plato

To enter life actually
Elbow tenoned soft
Tire market chipped tred
Trade talk for action jump
On this god-like venture

Heat

maneuver spelled
yanky 'sted of

chiefly british
artifice hums

within bridges
change works

hand a manual
operation awk

and burn out
first nation

feet trip
on Plymouth or

root just
rotten smoke

around the neck
just four things

to remember
and all of them

on the stove
all of them

back on the move

Heavy

That thought nothing between the beach and the pilings but the deep to disappearing talk under a dark north sky heaving its grey visible to penetrate the moment as *the* moment a larger south past an old cedar mind not quite lost but nearly petrified its headland shingled under winter's different prayers.

Household

no economy might appear
in the frost on the window

cedar outside radar
smell grinding

small bands of theory
written and restricted

dancing in the snow
of these interlake trails

stroked at ice
beard instead of breath

would that be sulphur
symmetry heard itself glyphed

sand, coded ice
the coke just shale

weight of the snow pack
local polis etched and stacked

only shade stenciled for track
breathing spending

breathing saving
whose nose has invested

evergreens and winter
this is the plan

and the body

In Sensed Truth

The sparrow's impasse in silence
crossed but not crossed
suspended
inserted
initialized

Back home the habit's tension
another true world born
mixed
      pre-natural

A tornado flaunts
silence

Over the mesa, under a calm blue
a black bird
tracks a stranger across the frame.

Kaslo

the clave of Cuba
sans drummer
                    la danza
holds on
to the math of multiple history
                              snare
some Florida
as the neck listens
                    count
quick white
black mixed
the shore the rim
shot
        echoes
mountain keyed
and climbed.

Loki Sniffs the Floods

body waterlogged
subterranean dream
of becoming a piling

all sky and osprey
mist hackles for ears
paws not on but in

the sand. Fastened
to the driftwood
highline welcome

every north storm
whisper home
to the Kokanee

and celebrate
in perfect stillness
each calm lake.

Mark

Broom Cracking
Crow Raven
Ravens Crows
Every Asshole
Has His Karma

Memory Stick

Built into the carrot
Scrubbed on the half pound
And then she sees the leaves past your face.

Courting tricks too fast for repetition
She dangles the modifier thinking
Bed, it's time for bed.

Trust the digital to fall to pieces
Pail's sloshing over the rear axle
Just one more octave of sea to sea.

Neck Hold

cement to the source
dances over top of the forms

looking for the chemistry, clouds
covert at the spring

creek pipe a little rusty
within the back eddy all possibility

lake a Newfoundland of roots
cellar one log

cellar two rock
cellar three concrete

cellar four ties
walls plumb & proof

a clear track through to the peppermint tea
pour hums plane overhead

dreamt a good mix five or six to two
not always back to shoulders

la cort de zone
maybe not just the cable of thinking

at the base of the neck
some bird sets

Nose Hill

Grass language knows
       silent flower wind
no trembled flutter

north of joy
       anemone mundi mound
emble hair scab

grace oat keel
       none shingle sky
June naze puzzle

imported sweet awn
       cope tribe discont-
but abundant thrill

never rough hooked
       dream street springing
ocean grade panic

gammas gone north
       thread-through-needle
spoke troop boat

w/ as ex hill
       noon pond knot
having omph look

clusted node broom
       first minute pendul
city licorice grazed

boulevard finger zome
　　　tickled sweet pyramid
influoresces occur animal

then *gna* loop
　　　feathered gravel home
new lawns rivers.

Parapoetic Sink
for George

How libidinal is the fear of reading? Carves, beats, hits, wags, points. *that I may cease to be.* Physical performs textual as anatomical memory re-engages the heave and accumulates a distinct sound for the body *in* language, outside the utterance, utter reflection of a syllable on the move.

Eyes skyhook over the intonation patterns and the dressed-up body morphs alongside the words, slight allomorphs of fingers, *cloudy symbols*, lips, nose reciprocate the narrative displacement of an "I" we think we know.

Ritual trace. To shore up the sure whole text of the speaking spoken. *that I may never live.*

Whose life do the dots connect? Whose grain elevator of glossolalia? Whose granny? Whose grammar?

Right hand signs to the left ear the air of intention: the material male body in the shape of the poem, with antlers, *starr'd*, but not in tension with the text, composition as position, the alignment of the torso spelled.

His hand goes to his face to adjust his glasses, to stroke his mustache, to run his forefinger down the cleft of his upper lip, to tick the end of his nose; margin of the poem, the spine *may cease to be.*

Between the thumb and the forefinger *full ripen'd grain.* This gesture confirms the focus of the witness box, an obvious *prosthetic* aid to punctuation. *oh what ears we waste on one another's plaints.*

When all five fingertips meet in a cluster it means there is no gap between the inscription and the poem. *let me start the engine and release ... the music.* (a sure bet).

Navigate the ritual face of iteration *Before my pen has gleaned my teeming brain ...*

Pinned Hole in the Wall

peaked back so tall
ravine-like
raven flies a blue shirt

ribs to cross ribs
huckleberry stain
so late in the year
alpine wants flowers

dry August drone
of Tiananmen
huge corner of sky
blue cloud floats

slow across that plate
heaven's table
the uniform of awareness
empties the magnet

long ago the distances
true shirt of the north
through that hole
mind coloured to the east.

The Proof of the Crocus

She said that our skin goes to soma with touch fingering those leaves on the prairie floor past purple as the shape of salt lapse hand in mind with a toe-headed baby over to anemone alpine memory hand in hand with old paper-thin precision dialling our on-mode a slight rub our aura of ghost buds gyna'd past hand power through stem into night so summer heat toggles the nipples lifted into seed.

Railing

The word geese zones in above these deck railings I've just built, hover along the parallel absolute of the opposite shore.

The pilings come out of the lake bed at my blurry eyes older yet sure of the osprey, the nest, piling.

Goodbye water says moving, even waves.

Honks.

Science of Fall

(leaves broke down)
choice not this
indeterminate need
the absolute ship
just floated
twenty after "A9"

X equals
old frosty road taken

from the sound
the dry choke
each step still *corpus*
counts into end
might miss out on
October

Spring and All

before it fall
greeny dream with lakeside scene

blackened cedar
from the southern sun

cabin's stood
another one

Tap Tap

sub
liminal
small morning chop this
all night
slept
in the lake
lapped dream after dream
through the narrows
cousins' voices
that fish weir story
nervous of history
tap tap
listening for an echo
from the bottom of the lake
(an often-crossed point from travel
becomes more sacred)
moon
caps the weather
packs a measure
chirps apostrophe
scary

Thin at 8800

roots under eye
redress of earth
larch feeding the path
rippled walk forth

to heaven above noon
thin galaxy at 8800
tied to its own knots
pressure on outer cortex
scree slope beckons, beckons

how soon will the yellow peak
a simple crash through yolk
the speed past emerald
in minutes chrome

this is no order
the original is soon worn out
the gravel on this trail
precalculates
the manifold descent

Warp Body

does the hole in your hand
seem to be disappearing
caught in the wrap

Beethoven was not furious
when he wrote this
but you are when you play it

outside of the music
the Appalachian is calm
Canadian as the bract
beneath the flower

bracken
you're just the speed
and your brow is furrowed
beard too long
excited to be home
inured to slivers
caught at warp

Winter: 65th Year

the roads feel longer after 54
the age my father danced to
as he fell to the ballroom floor
dreaming of islands
mountains and oceans crossed

a final new bed for the back
a little pain behind our conversation

another winter full of night

its dark brightened by the snow
foot falls awkward, a hesitation

older but knowing no better
still in love, wanting
that good song to be sung
inging it ahead into the dark
beyond the high beam
hoping

Words for Prairie

nose for alfalfa
and sage hills
distant
dust behind
all that
the eye can

      daughter
you beside
me not looking,
looking

why get it
us just
right here?